# LEGENDS
## OF THE WEST

The Black Cowboys

Butch Cassidy

Wyatt Earp

The Gunslingers

Jesse James

Annie Oakley

LEGENDS OF THE WEST

# THE GUNSLINGERS

*John Wukovits*

CHELSEA HOUSE PUBLISHERS
Philadelphia

**CHELSEA HOUSE PUBLISHERS**
*Editorial Director* Richard Rennert
*Production Manager* Pamela Loos
*Art Director* Sara Davis
*Picture Editor* Judy Hasday

***Staff for* THE GUNSLINGERS**
*Senior Editor* John Ziff
*Editorial Assistant* Kristine Brennan
*Designer* Takeshi Takahashi
*Cover Design and Digital Illustration* Alison Burnside
*Picture Researcher* Alan Gottlieb

First Printing

1 3 5 7 9 8 6 4 2

**Library of Congress Cataloging-in-Publication Data**

Wukovits, John F., 1944-
    The gunslingers / John Wukovits.
        p. cm.—(Legends of the West)
Includes bibliographical references and index
Summary: Describes the exploits of some of the men in the Old West, including
John Wesley Hardin, Billy the Kid, "Doc" Holliday, and James Butler Hickok, who
earned reputations for being deadly with a gun.
    ISBN 0-7910-3872-6 (hc)
1. Outlaws—West (U.S.)—Biography—Juvenile literature. 2. West (U.S.)—Biography—Juvenile literature. 3. Frontier and pioneer life—West (U.S.)—Juvenile
literature. [1. Robbers and outlaws. 2. Frontier and pioneer life—West (U.S.) 3.
West (U.S.)—Biography.] I. Title. II. Series.
F594.W85 1996
978'.02—dc20                                                              96-43112
                                                                              CIP
                                                                               AC

# CONTENTS

★

# "I Will Have No Mercy"

The lifeless body lay on the floor of the Acme Saloon for more than two hours. While the curious ambled in for a look, patrons, clutching glasses of whiskey, stepped around the slain man and returned to their gambling tables. When someone finally ended the bizarre scene by dragging the corpse outside, few took notice.

Earlier, on the night of August 19, 1895, the victim had been drinking and shooting dice in the El Paso, Texas, establishment. Several times he had been heard bragging that he was going to kill two men: a policeman who had arrested his girlfriend, and the policeman's father, with whom he had a long-standing dispute. At about 11:00 the policeman's father entered the saloon and fired a shot into the back of the victim's head. Thus ended the life of John Wesley Hardin, the Wild West's most notorious gunslinger.

No one mourned Hardin's passing. During

*According to his own count, John Wesley Hardin, among the deadliest of all gunslingers, killed 40 men. One victim's offense was snoring too loudly.*

his 42 years he had, by his own count, killed 40 men, one allegedly for the offense of snoring too loudly.

The inglorious death of the man considered the fastest draw anywhere signaled if not the end, then at least the twilight, of the gunslingers' era. In the dusty streets and rowdy saloons of western towns, at gambling tables and on the open range, these men had practiced their deadly craft. Confident that their reflexes were quicker, their nerves steadier, their aim more accurate than anyone else's, they turned to the gun to solve problems and settle disputes. But as civilization gradually replaced lawlessness in even the most remote areas of the country, society could no longer tolerate the gunslingers' violent ways.

John Wesley Hardin was born on May 25, 1853, in Bonham, Texas. His father, a Methodist minister, named him after the founder of his religion, John Wesley.

Hardin's life, like that of numerous gunslingers, changed dramatically when the Civil War erupted in 1861 and ushered in a horrifying era of hatred, death, and destruction. Sympathizing with the slave owners of the South, Hardin developed a bitter contempt for Union troops and for President Abraham Lincoln, whom he would later label, in his autobiography, "a demon incarnate who was waging a relentless and cruel war on the South to rob her of her sacred rights."

When the war ended in defeat for the Confederacy, Northern soldiers occupied Texas, and Hardin's hatred intensified. In 1868, while visiting his uncle's plantation, he got into a fight with an ex-slave named Mage. After Hardin had bloodied and beaten him, Mage swore that he

would kill the 15-year-old. As Hardin was riding home, the former slave appeared on the road, brandishing a large stick and shouting insults. Hardin pulled a pistol from his waistband and fatally shot Mage three times in the chest.

Believing that he would never receive fair treatment from the authorities, Hardin hid on the ranch of nearby relatives. When he heard that three Union soldiers were approaching, he ambushed and killed the men. The youthful Hardin, already responsible for four deaths, vowed he would have "no mercy on men who wanted my body to torture and kill."

Hoping to build his reputation, Hardin—like all gunslingers in the West—set about perfecting his skills with a six-shooter. He spent hours

*"One riot, one Ranger," the saying went. Translation: The Texas Rangers prided themselves on being the toughest lawmen anywhere. Shown here is Company F of the Rangers' Frontier Batallion. When John Wesley Hardin gunned down Sheriff Charlie Webb in 1874, the hard-nosed Rangers set out to bring him to justice.*

practicing until he felt he could outdraw anyone, developing a unique style that he claimed
saved precious seconds. Hardin sewed two hol-
sters into his vest that pointed the gun butts
toward each other. When he reached for them,
he swung his arms in an arc across his chest
in a cross-draw. Hardin became so quick that
a man who allegedly witnessed him outgun five
opponents marveled, "That boy can handle a
pistol faster than a frog can lick flies."

He had to, for in a gunfight any hesitation
could mean death. Bat Masterson, a lawman
turned writer, described what it took to become
a gunslinger:

> To accustom his hands to the pistols of those days,
> the man who coveted a reputation started in early
> and practiced with them just as a card sharp prac-
> tices with his cards, as a shell game man drills his
> fingers to manipulate the elusive pea, or a juggler
> must practice to acquire proficiency. When he could
> draw, cock and fire all in one smooth lightning-quick
> movement, he could then detach his mind from that
> movement and concentrate on accuracy.

Hardin began to carve out his reputation,
leaving a trail of bloodshed in his path. On
Christmas Day, 1870, he won $600 in a poker
game from an outlaw named Jim Bradley. When
Hardin claimed that Bradley still owed him $5,
Bradley drew a knife and threatened him.
Because he was not wearing his guns, Hardin
had to leave the bar to the sound of scornful
laughter. But the humiliated youth met Bradley
in the street later that night, and in the ensu-
ing gunfight he shot his antagonist dead.

A month later, a circus roustabout and
Hardin went for their guns after a brief scuffle.
Before his pistol had cleared the holster, the
roustabout was dead. Only a fews days after

that shooting, Hardin killed a man who was trying to rob him.

Arrested for a killing he denied having committed, Hardin was being transported to Waco to stand trial when he escaped by murdering a guard and fleeing on horseback. He claimed that he also shot down three Union troopers who were sent to bring him back.

Later, two other Union troopers named Green Parramore and John Lackey were searching for Hardin in Smiley, Texas. Hardin approached the men and asked whether they knew what their quarry looked like. When they replied that they did not, he revealed that he was the feared outlaw. Before the troopers could react, Hardin's guns were drawn and he was pumping bullets into them. Parramore died; his partner was luckier, surviving serious wounds to tell his story.

As a result of these and other killings, John Wesley Hardin had by this time earned the reputation he cherished: that of a deadly gunslinger. He was only 18 years old.

But one of the ironies of seeking fame as a gunslinger was that once a man had gained it, he could not really relax and enjoy it. If lawmen were not on his trail, if relatives or friends of his victims were not bent on revenge, then the gunslinger still had to worry about the ambitious young challengers lurking in the shadows, ready to kill or be killed to establish *their* reputations.

Hardin fell into the pattern that defined the lives of most of the gunslingers. He drifted from town to town, generally using aliases to conceal his identity. But wherever he traveled, he was a marked man.

"In those days," Hardin later explained, "my life was constantly in danger from secret or hired assassins, and I was always on the lookout."

*After fellow Texas Ranger John Duncan had intercepted a letter revealing Hardin's whereabouts, Captain John Armstrong (shown here) captured the gunslinger on a train in Pensacola, Florida. When Hardin attempted to draw his guns, Armstrong knocked him out with the butt of his pistol.*

Texas Rangers, Pinkerton detectives, and sheriffs scoured the nation for the gunslinger, who vowed "never to surrender at the muzzle of a gun."

In one town, a man burst into Hardin's hotel room and threatened to kill him. Hardin pulled some money out of his pants to calm his confronter and, as he handed it over, let some coins drop to the floor. He later boasted that the man "stooped down to pick them up and as he was straightening up I pulled my pistol and fired. The ball struck him between the eyes and he fell over." Hardin had to make a speedy exit before the law came for him.

At times Hardin tried to make special arrangements with the town sheriff, especially if that man also happened to be a noted gunslinger. When Hardin stopped at Abilene, Kansas, one of the first things he did was arrange a truce with its lawman, Wild Bill Hickok. Being noted gunmen, the two understood each other in a way that others could not. In return for good behavior by Hardin, Hickok promised to leave him alone during his stay in Abilene.

But the truce did not last. Supposedly angered over a man's loud snoring from the hotel room next to his, the gunslinger pumped a number of bullets through the thin wall, killing the unfortunate snorer. Knowing that Hickok would soon be after him and "would kill me to add to his reputation," Hardin had to hustle out of Abilene.

In Trinity City, Texas, Hardin suckered a gunman named Phil Sublett into a bowling match and proceeded to take all his money. Sublett later burst into the town's saloon, where Hardin was drinking, and blasted him with a shotgun. Hardin staggered out into the street and gunned the fleeing Sublett down before collapsing.

While recovering from his wounds at a deserted ranch, Hardin was surprised by two lawmen who fired through a window as he lay on a bed. The gunslinger took a bullet in the thigh but managed to reach a shotgun and drive off his attackers.

Amazingly, Hardin found time to marry his longtime sweetheart, Jane Bowen, in 1872. Like many gunslingers who lived through a seemingly endless cycle of murders and hasty escapes, of constant danger and gruesome savagery, Hardin thirsted for moments of normalcy. But his status as the most notorious gunslinger in Texas ensured that the couple would never enjoy a peaceful life together. Their brief moments of togetherness were separated by long periods when Hardin lived on the run.

As his reputation grew even larger, more and more people tried to bring Hardin down. In 1874 Sheriff Charlie Webb learned that Hardin was staying in nearby Comanche, Texas, under an agreement with the local lawman. He traveled to Comanche to arrest the gunslinger, whom he encountered outside a saloon. Hardin asked whether Webb had papers for his arrest. When the lawman answered no, he invited Webb into the saloon for a drink.

As Hardin strolled into the saloon, a friend yelled, "Look out!" Webb, who had drawn on him from behind, managed to get off a shot that hit Hardin in the side. But the sheriff was probably already dead, as Hardin had spun around, pulled his pistols, and fired a bullet into his head in one lightning-fast movement. According to Hardin's count, Webb was the 40th man he had killed. Wounded, but not critically, Hardin rode out of town.

The killing of Sheriff Webb, a popular lawman, provoked outrage throughout Texas. For three years various agencies, including the Texas Rangers and the Pinkerton Detective Agency, carried on a massive manhunt for Hardin, who had fled to Florida and was living under the name J. H. Swain. They finally located him when Texas Ranger John Duncan, posing as a farmhand on a ranch owned by Hardin's relatives, intercepted a family letter revealing Hardin's whereabouts. On August 23, 1877, Texas Ranger

John B. Armstrong met a train at the Pensaco-la, Florida, station. Spotting his quarry inside the train, Armstrong cautiously boarded, drew his pistol, and approached the outlaw's seat.

Hardin saw the lawman and tried to pull out his guns, but they became entangled in his suspenders, causing an amused Armstrong to recall that the outlaw "almost pulled his breeches over his head" trying to free his weapons. Armstrong scurried up and knocked Hardin unconscious with his pistol.

During his trial for Webb's murder, Hardin—who pleaded his own case—displayed a characteristic of most gunslingers: the tendency to shift blame for every killing to someone else. He told the jury that he "never shot a man except in self-defense." Other gunslingers sought to justify their violent acts by blaming "evil" authorities, money-hungry big businesses, or their war experiences.

This jury was not swayed, however. It found Hardin guilty of second-degree murder, and the judge sentenced him to 25 years' hard labor at the feared Huntsville, Texas, prison.

Seventeen years later, Hardin emerged from prison to an entirely different world. His wife had died two years earlier, and the days of Wild West gunslingers had largely faded into memory. Hardin, who had spent his last years in prison studying law, claimed to have completely reformed. But he soon began drinking heavily and brawling, and his threats to kill policeman John Selman and his father, John, Sr., led to his own ignominious death on an El Paso saloon floor.

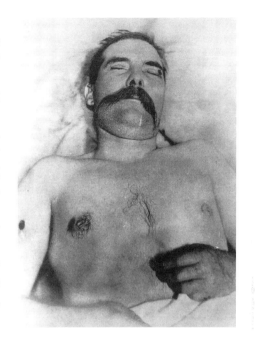

*John Wesley Hardin in death. The mark above his left eyelid is an exit wound from the first—and fatal—shot that John Selman, Sr., fired. Taking no chances, Selman squeezed off two more shots as the gunslinger lay on the floor, producing the wounds visible on Hardin's right arm and chest.*

# "They Fought Because They Wanted to Fight"

hen someone asked the notorious gunslinger Clay Allison what his profession
was, he responded, "I am a shootist."
Allison's description, though perhaps a bit
self-aggrandizing, is revealing. The men who
became gunslingers considered themselves a
breed apart from the rest—they believed they
possessed special qualities that elevated them
above "ordinary" gunmen.

On the basis of practice alone, they certainly were in a class by themselves, for gunslingers
worked hard to fine-tune their skills and become
not simply the fastest draw, but also the most
accurate shot. First, they had to master the com-

*Deadwood, Dakota Territory, in 1876, the year gun-
slinger Turkey Creek Jack Johnson shot and killed
two gunmen in a celebrated showdown near the
town cemetery. That same year Deadwood witnessed the demise of another famous gunslinger:
Wild Bill Hickok.*

plicated move of simultaneously drawing a six-shooter out of its holster, stretching the trigger finger down at a 45-degree angle to the trigger, and lifting the thumb to cock the hammer. This is where speed became important.

Second—and most gunslingers believed this aspect was more critical than speed—they had to become accurate shooters, a skill that required concentration. The famous lawman Wyatt Earp claimed that the gunslinger who survived a shoot-out was usually the one who took his time. He explained that a gunfight required "going into action with the greatest speed of which a man's muscles are capable, but mentally unflustered by an urge to hurry. . . ." A gunslinger needed quickness to get the gun out of its holster, then controlled, accurate shooting, especially since many gunfights occurred with the opponents no more than 10 or 20 yards apart.

Gunslingers also had to know when to draw and when not to draw. Going to the gun too quickly could result in unnecessary bloodshed, but hesitating to draw could also speedily end a gunslinger's career. It boiled down to instinct. Wild Bill Hickok took time—a split second at most—to judge whether his foe required facing down or gunning down. He advised, "Whenever you get into a row [a fight] be sure and not shoot too quick.  Take time. I've known many a feller slip up for shootin' in a hurry."

Another gunslinger, Jim Moon, claimed he could instantly evaluate a man. "The man who pulls a gun on you when you have nothing in sight is a cur," Moon declared. "All you need to do is walk right up to him, take it away and beat him over the head with it, so he won't try it again."

Noted gunslingers rarely faced each other, and even went out of their way to avoid confrontations. During one visit to Wild Bill Hickok's Abilene, Jesse and Frank James sent word to the marshal that they intended to break no law, but if Hickok came out to challenge them, they would arrange for his funeral. Hickok kept a respectful distance from the outlaws.

Instead, gunslingers had to deal with the numerous "young guns" who wanted to earn a reputation by besting an established gunfighter, or they resorted to gunplay when someone cheated them or their honor was at stake. Once in motion, gunfights became practically impossible to stop.

One Dodge City newspaper printed a story in 1879 about two men determined to fight over a woman:

> Both, or either of these men, we believe, might have avoided this shooting if either had possessed a desire to do so. But both being willing to risk their lives, each with confidence in himself, they fought because they wanted to fight.

As a result, one of the men died.

Though most gunfights did not involve two men walking and firing straight at each other, as Hollywood movies lead us to believe, many celebrated incidents took place in that manner. In an 1876 confrontation in Deadwood, Dakota Territory, for example, Turkey Creek Jack Johnson illustrated the value of calmness and steady shooting. After getting into an argument with two men, Johnson challenged them to shoot it out. Each of his adversaries strapped on two six-shooters, then lined up 50 yards away on a road that, appropriately, skirted the town cemetery. As the duo stepped toward him, Johnson patiently waited. Before they had paced 10 yards, the two inexperienced gunmen had each emptied one revolver's worth of bullets and switched to the second.

With his gun drawn but not raised, the unharmed Johnson walked toward his foes while bullets whizzed by his head. When he stepped within 30 yards of the men, Johnson slowly raised his six-shooter and killed one man with his first shot. He then waited while the second man fired three more shots, all wide of their target, then dropped him with a second bullet.

Hickok shot down Davis Tutt in another famous gunfight, which took place in 1865 in Springfield, Missouri. During a card game, Tutt claimed that Hickok owed him money, and when the two men disagreed on the amount, he reached across the table and seized a prized watch that Hickok had been given by his mother. When Tutt boasted that he would wear the watch the following day in the town square—a boast designed to provoke—Hickok warned him that such an act would be unwise.

The next day at about 6:00 P.M., both men

*The 1873 Colt Peacemaker, pistol of choice for many gunslingers, was dubbed "the weapon that won the West." Among those who staked their lives on its reliability was Wyatt Earp (opposite page), whose stints as a lawman took him to such dangerous towns as Wichita and Dodge City, Kansas, and Tombstone, Arizona.*

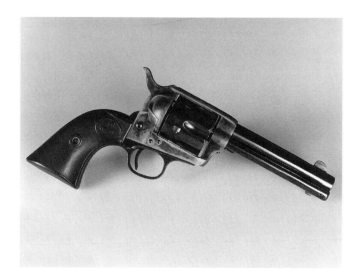

appeared at the square in the middle of town. From 100 yards apart, they began walking toward each other, firing their six-shooters as they moved. One of Hickok's bullets tore into Tutt's chest and killed him instantly. Hickok was later tried for manslaughter but found not guilty.

Gunslingers favored certain types of weapons. Dominating the handgun field were the various Colt pistols, especially the Colt Peacemaker of 1873, more commonly known as the Colt .45, which some have called the weapon that won the West. Less likely to misfire than earlier versions, the Colt had an effective range of 100 yards.

Wyatt Earp, Ben Thompson, Pat Garrett, and Billy the Kid all carried Colts. The gun, a single-action, six-shot handgun that gave rise to the term *six-shooter*, proved so popular that westerners liked to say, "God created men; Colonel Colt made them equal." One El Paso man swore, "I would as soon go out into the street without my pants as without my Colt."

When the Colt company adapted the Peacemaker so that it fired the same-size shells used by the Winchester rifle, the gun practically eliminated all competition. Now each man would have to buy only one kind of shell for both his six-shooter and rifle.

Besides his six-shooter, a gunslinger usually carried a rifle for longer distance. The Winchester Model 1873, with its 12- or 15-shot versions, dominated the field. According to Buffalo Bill Cody, Indians would give more in trade for a Winchester than for any other gun. When employees of a rival rifle factory went on strike, a newspaper report stated that the workers who refused to join the strike walked into the factory with "their trusty Winchesters."

When the fighting moved to extremely close range, the small derringer came into play. A single- or double-shot pistol, the derringer carried such force that at close ranges of 10 to 20 feet, it could blow a huge hole in a man. Since the gun could easily be hidden on a person, derringers were used by gamblers, con artists, and women as well as by gunslingers.

Though few of them lived to enjoy old age and a peaceful death, gunslingers generally made no attempt to change their life-styles. They fit comfortably into the rough conditions of the Wild West. For most people, civilization was a blessing; not so for the gunslinger. In 1879 the

*Dodge City Globe* reported that gunslingers looked "with horror upon the approach of manners, customs and ideas tending to drive out the 'frontier' characteristics of Dodge. They look with profound contempt upon a town whose police officers are not walking arsenals."

As civilization inched westward, the gunslingers who remained found their way of life increasingly out of step with the society around them. By the turn of the century, the Wild West was no longer quite so wild, and there was simply no room anymore for these most violent of men.

# "I See Mighty Few Friends"

**A**lthough virtually everyone on the frontier owned firearms, the gunslingers' skill gave them a distinct advantage in their dealings with others. And many of them used this advantage to get away with illegal activities. Among the more prominent of these men were Billy the Kid, William Longley, and Doc Holliday.

Many of the details of his early life are unknown or disputed, but the infamous outlaw who came to be called Billy the Kid is believed to have been born in a New York City slum on November 23, 1859. His name was probably William H. Bonney (although some authorities believe it was Henry McCarty). After his father died while Billy was still a youth, he and his

*John Henry "Doc" Holliday was a vicious dentist-turned-gunslinger who frequently ran afoul of the law. Nevertheless, he formed a lasting friendship with Wyatt Earp, a respected lawman, and stood by Earp during the gunfight at the O. K. Corral.*

mother and brother moved west. Mrs. Bonney, who was described as "a jolly Irish lady, full of life and mischief," remarried in 1873, and the family settled in Silver City, New Mexico.

Apparently no one noticed anything unusual about Billy at this time. A teacher stated that he was "no more of a problem than any other boy, always quite willing to help with chores around the schoolhouse."

Billy's mother died of tuberculosis in 1874, when Billy was 15. The youth rarely left his mother's side during her final four-month illness, tenderly holding her in his arms when severe coughing spells wracked her frail body. After her death, Billy came into conflict with his stepfather, William Antrim, and left Silver City.

His first recorded killing took place three years later in Grant City, Arizona, the initial sordid act in a four-year spree of murder. (Stories that Billy had previously committed various murders are unsubstantiated.) In Grant City, a blacksmith named Cahill seems to have taunted and bullied the 17-year-old relentlessly. On August 17, 1877, as Cahill was roughing him up in a saloon, Billy pulled a gun and shot him. It was from this incident that his nickname, the Kid, arose; he looked too young to be a killer.

Fleeing the law, Billy ended up in Lincoln County, New Mexico, where he worked on the cattle ranch of John Tunstall, an Englishman he came to idolize. For his part, Tunstall saw great promise in Billy, telling others that the young man was "quick to learn and not afraid of anything." He gave Billy a new horse, saddle, and gun. Before long Tunstall had become a father figure to the troubled youth.

In 1878 a bitter feud between rival cattle

*William Bonney was 17 and an obscure ranch hand when he posed for this portrait. Within a year the young killer had earned the nickname by which he is familiar even today: Billy the Kid.*

concerns erupted into what became known as the Lincoln County War. The county's entrenched cattle barons regarded newcomers such as Tunstall as threats to their economic interests. Those men, led by Lawrence Murphy and James Dolan, were determined to use whatever means necessary to prevent Tunstall from expanding his operations. When harassment and intimidation failed, the Murphy-Dolan faction murdered Tunstall on February 18.

A shaken Billy promised to avenge his friend's death, and before a month had passed the first killings in retaliation had occurred. The county ran with blood as each side set ambushes and attacked the other with such fury that President Rutherford B. Hayes appointed a special governor, Lew Wallace, to bring order to the area.

Billy, who played a central part in many of the killings—including the execution of two Murphy-Dolan gunmen he was supposed to have been helping transport to face justice and the ambush of a sheriff—decided to make a deal with the governor. In return for testifying against three men he had seen murder a lawyer, Billy would receive a full pardon for his crimes. He would still have to stand trial for the killing of the sheriff, but Governor Wallace promised to set him free regardless of the verdict. After giving his testimony, Billy slipped away before his trial had begun.

Enraged that Billy had failed to live up to his end of the bargain, the governor placed a $500 reward on his head. Billy, meanwhile, had organized a gang of outlaws and was engaged in horse and cattle theft.

When Pat Garrett, a former friend of Billy's, was appointed sheriff of Lincoln County in early 1880, he immediately started hunting for the outlaw. He had no success until December, when he learned that Billy would be riding near Fort Sumner, an abandoned army post that an associate of Billy's, Pete Maxwell, used as a ranch. Garrett and his posse set a trap, and on December 18, Billy and four of his gang rode into it. In the furious gun battle, Garrett's posse killed Billy's friend Tom O'Folliard, but the others escaped.

The tenacious sheriff stuck to Billy's trail. On December 26, Garrett and his men surrounded Billy's gang in an adobe hut at Stink-

ing Springs and forced them to surrender by simply waiting until they had run out of food. Billy was taken to Mesilla in southern New Mexico, where a jury found him guilty of murder and sentenced him to hang in Lincoln on May 13, 1881.

Garrett and a group of guards carefully transported Billy the Kid to Lincoln and placed him in the top floor of the Lincoln County Courthouse. In the weeks before the scheduled execution, newspaper reporters flocked to the courthouse to interview the condemned man. Like other gunslingers, Billy welcomed the opportunity to add to his fame, and he also offered some well-worn excuses for his criminal behavior. He was a victim—persecuted because he stood up to the powerful cattlemen in Lincoln County, singled out even though many men deserved to hang more than he. "It's wrong," he whined, "that I should be the only

*This illustration from Pat Garrett's 1882 book,* An Authentic Life of Billy the Kid, *may contain some fanciful elements— the room was actually pitch black, for example—but it gives a pretty good idea of how the Kid met his end on July 14, 1881.*

*Sheriff Pat Garrett achieved a measure of fame himself when he shot and killed his former buddy, the legendary Billy the Kid.*

one to suffer the extreme penalties of the law."

Garrett had assigned two men, deputies Bob Ollinger and James Bell, to guard Billy on the top floor of the courthouse. On April 28 they relaxed just enough to give Billy the chance to escape the hangman.

While Ollinger ate lunch in a restaurant across the street, Bell brought some food to the prisoner. When he removed the handcuff from Billy's left wrist so the young outlaw could eat, Billy lunged toward Bell, knocked him hard across the forehead with the dangling handcuff, grabbed the deputy's gun, and killed him.

Ollinger heard the gunshot and rushed back to the courthouse, but by then Billy had gotten his hands on a shotgun. Before Ollinger stepped into the building, Billy murdered him with a blast from the weapon.

Still shackled, but armed now with two six-shooters and a Winchester rifle, Billy remained at the building for an hour, taunting everyone who drew within hearing range. One witness later told Garrett, who was out of town on business, "The Kid was all over the building, on the porch, watching from the windows. He danced about the balcony, laughed and shouted as though he had not a care on earth."

Billy finally decided he had pressed his luck far enough. He hobbled out of the building to a blacksmith shop, where he ordered a blacksmith at gunpoint to remove his shackles. Once free, Billy stole a horse and raced out of town.

When Garrett returned, he quickly formed another posse and set out in hot pursuit. Acting on information that Billy had a girlfriend at Fort Sumner, Garrett surrounded the ranch house with his deputies on July 14, 1881. He waited until after dark, but when he detected no sign of his quarry, he entered.

Billy, apparently having heard a noise outside, suddenly appeared on the front porch. Deputies in hiding did not recognize him, but while Billy was on the porch Garrett found his way into a darkened bedroom. When Billy

walked back inside the house and into the bedroom, he sensed that someone was there. He
asked who it was, but two bullets from Garrett's
gun cut him short. The infamous murderer, only
21 years old, slumped dead to the floor, his four-
year career as an outlaw finally ended.

As with many western gunslingers, legends
quickly arose about the life of Billy the Kid. Within a year of his death, eight novels selling over
one million copies had made him into a hero
and "credited" him with killing 21 men, "one for
every year of my life," as the outlaw used to
boast. Though the actual figure is probably
lower—maybe eight or nine—readers accepted
the larger number, like much of the Kid's legend, as truth. Billy was often described sym-
pathetically, as an unfortunate youth who
turned to crime only after the tragic loss of both
parents and a father figure. But in reality he
was little more than a ruthless murderer who
could not adjust to the norms of society.

Pat Garrett, who knew Billy quite well and
frequently saw the outlaw's warm smile, accu-
rately summed up his callous disregard for
human life. "Those who knew him best," Garrett declared, "will tell you that in his most savage and dangerous moods his face always wore
a smile. He ate and laughed, drank and laughed,
rode and laughed, talked and laughed, fought
and laughed—and killed and laughed."

One man who rarely laughed—and who
equalled or surpassed the terror spread by Billy
the Kid—was William P. Longley. Born on August
6, 1851, in Austin County, Texas, Longley early
built a reputation as a bully. Violence seemed
to follow in his wake, and by the time he was
15, the brown-eyed, black-haired youth had
killed his first man.

*"Hanging is my favorite way of dying," gunslinger William P. Longley (center) declared. Shortly after this photo was taken, the 27-year-old, responsible for as many as 32 killings, faced the gallows.*

Like many other killers who roamed the West, Longley firmly believed that the South had been cruelly treated following the Civil War. To avenge the South's honor, he turned to killing, especially blacks or people who sympathized with the North.

A black lawman was his first victim. Appointed by the Northern occupation government, the lawman boldly rode down the street of Longley's hometown, waving a rifle and ordering local whites out of his way. Longley obstructed his path and warned him to stop threatening whites,

but when the lawman took his time respond-
ing, Longley gunned him down. Townspeople,
who approved of Longley's action, buried the
victim and let the matter quietly go away.

Life on the move appealed to Longley, who
never felt comfortable around too many people.
He worked as a cowboy, field hand, and gam-

bler, drifting to Arkansas, Kansas, Wyoming, Dakota Territory, and Indian Territory.

He seemed in his element in the wilds of the West, particularly in the Black Hills of Dakota, where he operated a saloon. "There was no law at all," he later explained. "It was simply the rule of claw and tooth and fang. . . . "

*Tombstone, Arizona, site of the famous gunfight at the O. K. Corral.*

Longley was known as a quick draw, so in addition to the gunfights he instigated, he faced numerous gunmen who hoped to make their reputations by killing him. None succeeded.

In 1875 one of Longley's cousins was ambushed by a Texas rancher named Wilson Anderson, who had feuded with the Longley family for years. Hearing of the killing, Longley returned to Texas and murdered Anderson.

The Texas Rangers immediately set out to bring Longley to justice, which forced him to flee to Louisiana. He continued his murderous ways in that state, successfully evading the law until the dogged Rangers closed in and captured him on May 13, 1877. After a speedy trial in Giddings, Texas, concluded with a guilty verdict, the judge sentenced Longley to be hanged.

Longley spent his final days corresponding with various people and talking about his life. He complained in writing to the governor of Texas about what he considered unfair treatment—John Wesley Hardin had received only a long prison sentence for his killings, yet Longley was condemned to die. He asked the governor why, but the governor did not respond.

Longley frequently chatted with his guards, who recalled that the prisoner expressed no regrets over killing as many as 32 people. When one guard asked how he had avoided capture for years, Longley responded, "I never had any confidence in nobody."

Longley remained hardened to the end. In a letter to a girl shortly before his death, he declared, "Hanging is my favorite way of dying." When he stepped up to the gallows on October 11, 1878, and gazed upon the huge crowd of 4,000 who had gathered to witness his execution, Longley muttered to the hangman, "I see a good many enemies around, and mighty few friends." Seconds later the trapdoor opened, and the 27-year-old killer fell to his death.

John Henry Holliday, known to history as Doc Holliday, was a complex man. Despite being one of the quickest guns and most ruthless outlaws in the West, he maintained an unshakable loyalty to a lawman, Wyatt Earp.

Born in Griffin, Georgia, in 1852, Holliday studied dentistry at a Baltimore college of dental surgery and set up practice in Atlanta in 1872. But severe coughing bouts from tuberculosis forced him to travel west in search of a warmer, drier climate. While in Texas, Holliday murdered his first man and began a life of drifting from one western cow town to another, gambling, drinking, chasing women—and picking fights.

Early on, Holliday realized that his frailness was an obstacle in the West, where violent men held sway. According to lawman Bat Masterson, "Physically, Doc Holliday was a weakling who could not have whipped a healthy 15-year-old boy in a fist fight." To remedy this disadvantage, Holliday honed his gun-handling skills until they stood second to none. Wyatt Earp, who had seen hundreds of gunslingers in his day, declared that Holliday was "the nerviest, speediest, deadliest man with a six-gun that I ever knew." Others claimed that the little dentist, who was able to shoot with either hand, could hit two opponents with two shots before they got off one.

Such skill became even more dangerous combined with Holliday's foul temper. He was normally irritable, Masterson wrote, but "under the influence of liquor was a most dangerous man." He took offense easily and was always ready to shoot anyone whose pride stood in the way of a cringing apology for a nonexistent slight. People joked grimly that Holliday was well "drilled in the art of dentistry, but for those who doubted his ability, he would drill 'em for free." His reputation so spread that the *Denver Republican* wrote, "For years he has roamed the West, gaining his living by gambling, robbery and murder. In the Southwest his name is a terror."

Violence followed in Holliday's path, most frequently started by the sickly dentist. In 1876 he killed a soldier of the Sixth U.S. Cavalry in Texas over a gambling quarrel and had to flee. He eventually landed in Fort Griffin, Texas, where he first met Wyatt Earp, who was tracking a criminal. Their friendship developed into a deep attachment that astounded most of Earp's other associates.

After Holliday killed another man while in Fort Griffin, he was arrested and, in the absence of a jail, locked in a hotel room. Many of the angry townspeople wanted to lynch him, but with the help of a female accomplice named Big-Nose Kate Elder, he escaped.

Holliday roamed the mining and cattle towns that sprinkled the West, where he could find easy marks for his gambling. Eventually he wound up in Tombstone, Arizona. There Wyatt Earp and his brothers had established themselves as lawmen and successful businessmen.

A powerful group of cattle rustlers known as the Clanton-McLowery gang, headed by Ike Clanton, wanted to rid Tombstone of the Earps. Tension mounted until on October 26, 1881, near the O. K. Corral, the two sides met in a brief but brutal gunfight that left three men dead and three wounded.

Holliday stood at Wyatt Earp's side through

the crisis. At first the lawman tried to keep his friend out of it by telling him shortly before the battle, "Doc, this is our fight. There's no call for you to mix in." Holliday informed Earp that he had no intention of abandoning him now, and he was offended at the mere suggestion that he do so.

The half-minute gunfight is one of the most celebrated shoot-outs in the history of the West. As bullets screamed by and smoke filled the air, Holliday calmly shot at the rival gunmen from close distance, wounding at least one man while suffering a hip wound himself. Though the Earp faction killed three of the Clanton-McLowery gang and technically emerged victorious, Ike Clanton refused to let the feud end. He organized attacks on the Earps, which resulted in the murder of one of Wyatt's brothers and the serious wounding of another.

Holliday continued his reckless ways after leaving Tombstone, even though his health deteriorated. Horrible coughing spells occurred more often and left him as limp as a rag. Though only 36, the feeble dentist looked like an old man. Finally, in May 1887, Holliday entered a sanatorium in Glenwood Springs, Colorado, where he died on November 8, 1887.

# "RULE OF IRON"

Though the term suggests lawlessness, gunslingers could be found on both sides of the law. In fact, it is sometimes difficult to characterize a given gunslinger as either law-abiding or outlaw, for he may one day have ridden with a legally formed posse and the next day shot a man during an argument over cards. Or he may at one point in his career have worn a badge but later turned to crime. Or he may have used his badge simply to enrich himself or settle scores with enemies. In short, the line between legality and illegality was frequently blurred in the Wild West.

James Butler Hickok was a gunslinger known primarily as a lawman. Born May 27, 1837, in Troy Grove, Illinois, Hickok, like many gunslingers, traveled west to escape trouble. In 1855 he got into a savage fight with a fellow laborer and erroneously thought he had killed the man, so he headed for St. Louis.

*James Butler "Wild Bill" Hickok, 1871. As a marshal, the fearless gunslinger cleaned up some of the most lawless towns in the West.*

After a short stint as a stagecoach driver, he joined the Union forces as a scout and spy during the Civil War. According to some accounts, he earned the nickname "Wild Bill" for his wartime exploits; other accounts assert that the nickname was bestowed when Hickok defended his friend from a lynch mob by stepping in front of the mob, drawing his gun, and warning, "Leave or there will be more dead men around here than the town can bury." As the intimidated mob turned and left, a woman shouted, "Good for you, Wild Bill!"

Hickok alternated between scouting for the army and law enforcement after the Civil War. In 1866 he met the renowned newspaper correspondent H. M. Stanley while acting as deputy U.S. marshal at Fort Riley, Kansas. Stanley's highly flattering article propelled Hickok's reputation to new heights—and made him a target for toughs and young gunmen.

The next year he walked into a Nebraska bar, weary and dirty from a hard day's riding. Four men taunted him so unmercifully that he slapped one across the face. The other three reached for their guns, but within seconds Hickok had drawn and shot each of the three assailants. He suffered only a slight arm wound in the scuffle.

Two years later Hickok took the job of marshal in Hays City, Kansas, a rough town located near the army post at Fort Hays, then the home of General George Armstrong Custer's Seventh Cavalry. He quickly informed Hays City's inhabitants that he intended to keep the peace by whatever means needed and that they should behave. One acquaintance recalled, "When Wild Bill ruled in the name of good citizenship it fared ill with every pistol expert who

undertook to run the town." Hays City residents learned that their new lawman meant business.

Hickok rarely bothered anyone for minor reasons, but if a tough threatened him, he wasted little time answering the challenge. The *Hays City Sentinel* wrote that

> when Bill was once convinced of an adequate cause for taking a hand in a row, there was always a funeral. This is where he differed from the generality of frontiersmen. The ordinary ruffian, when involved in a row, would bluster around until, in the natural course of events, he would get shot; while Bill would perforate his opponent and then do his blustering at the funeral.

A man named Sullivan learned this the hard way. Wishing to earn his own reputation by shooting Hickok, Sullivan leaped out of an alley

*Abilene, Kansas, was the end of the line for many a cattle drive. After weeks or even months on the trail, the cowboys were in desperate need of some entertainment—and they tended to favor a distinctively rowdy variety. In Abilene's numerous saloons and brothels, brawls and shootings were daily occurrences, and the violence frequently spilled into the streets, making the town one of the most dangerous in the West. Beginning in 1871, Wild Bill Hickok patrolled Abilene's dusty streets as town marshal.*

with a six-shooter pointed at the lawman.

"I got you, Hickok. Now I'm going to kill you," he boasted. But the foolish gunman was not content merely to kill the famous gunslinger; he also wanted an audience. While he shouted for a crowd to witness the demise of Wild Bill Hickok, he failed to notice Hickok quietly inching his hand toward his gun. In a swift motion, Hickok whipped his six-shooter out of its holster and killed Sullivan with one shot.

"He talked his life away," the lawman commented afterward.

Hickok had to leave Hays City abruptly following a fracas with members of the Seventh Cavalry. Angered that he had arrested a group of soldiers for disturbing the peace, seven cavalrymen rode into Hays City to get revenge. They located Hickok in a saloon, but a brief fight left one soldier dead and another badly wounded. Fearing that other members of Custer's unit would come for him, Hickok boarded a train for Ellsworth, Kansas.

Abilene, Kansas, one of the largest and wildest cow towns in the West, next beckoned. In April 1871 Hickok took the job of town marshal and again let people know he would do whatever was necessary to make the town safe for decent citizens.

Cattle baron Joseph McCoy described Hickok's tenure in Abilene as "a rule of iron . . . There was no fooling with the courts of the law. . . . Wild Bill cleaned up the town and kept it clean. But [he] had to kill a few roughs to do it."

Like many gunslingers, Hickok presented a fierce sight in public. He patrolled the streets armed to the teeth: his six-shooter in his hip holster, a huge bowie knife stuck in his belt, derringers hidden under his coat, a rifle or shot-gun cradled in his arm. Only the foolish thought about challenging him.

His fame increased with each account of his exploits. Correspondents from eastern news-papers loved interviewing Hickok because he always sent them away with a good story, even if he strayed a bit from the truth. And Hickok, for his part, loved the attention.

Comments from such notable figures as Gen-eral Custer, for whom Hickok had scouted, fur-ther added to his reputation. Custer proclaimed:

> Whether on foot or on horseback he was one of the most perfect types of physical manhood I ever saw. Of his courage there could be no question: it has been brought to the test on too many occasions to doubt. His skill in the use of the rifle and pistol was unerring.

Amazingly, Hickok faced few problems from other noted gunslingers. Whenever their paths crossed, an uneasy pact allowed both parties to peacefully coexist. In return for their good behav-ior in his town, the marshal would leave the gunslingers alone. At one time or another, Hickok encountered Jesse and Frank James, Ben Thompson, and John Wesley Hardin, all without bloodshed. His trouble came from unknowns attempting to make their careers.

Hickok became so worried about being mur-dered while he slept that he spread newspapers on his floor. In that way he could detect any-body trying to enter the room by the rustling sound they would create. He carefully checked every door and window; he avoided sleeping wherever there might be an open line of fire. He may not have had to live on the run, as did gun-slingers like Jesse James and Billy the Kid, but he had to live with constant danger.

Hickok's worries were not limited to the nighttime. One writer who knew the lawman stated that he

> would never enter a place and walk up the middle of the floor, or turn his back to the door. His mode of entry was to step swiftly across the threshold of a room and move to one side so that nobody who saw him enter could shoot him from the outside. Next, standing close to the wall, he would survey the room, noting every person in it. Then he would make his way along the wall to the bar or wherever he desired to go.

Fame as a gunslinger carried a heavy price.

In October 1871, while investigating a gunshot outside an Abilene saloon, Hickok confronted a dozen gunmen, including an old adversary named Phil Coe. When Hickok ordered him to hand over his guns, Coe responded by firing two shots at the marshal. Hickok fired back, fatally wounding Coe. But when Hickok's friend Mike Williams saw the commotion and raced to the marshal's aid, Hickok, mistaking him for one of the gunmen, shot him in the head, killing him instantly.

Despondent over the accidental shooting of his friend, Hickok resigned his position as marshal and left Abilene in December 1871. It is believed that he never again fired a gun at a man.

By the summer of 1876, Hickok was in Deadwood, Dakota Territory. Deadwood, a wild mining town of 25,000, featured numerous saloons and gambling tables. There Wild Bill Hickok met his end when Jack McCall, an unknown who hoped to carve a name out of killing a noted gunslinger, walked into the Number Ten Saloon on August 2, 1876, spotted Hickok playing cards, and shot him in the back of the head.

Hickok, who never knew what hit him, slumped forward and died, holding onto a pair of aces and a pair of eights—forever after known among poker players as "the dead man's hand."

While frantic townspeople shouted, "Wild Bill is shot! Wild Bill is shot!" a group of settlers captured McCall. When a miners' court of law astonishingly acquitted the gunman of murder, McCall quickly rode out of town to avoid being lynched. But, like many a true gunslinger—which he certainly was not—McCall could not resist the lure of fame. Instead of quietly blending into his surroundings, he repeatedly bragged about how he had shot Wild Bill Hickok. In August he was arrested and again forced to stand trial for murder, the first verdict having been nullified because the trial had taken place on Indian land rather than on U.S. soil. This time McCall was found guilty. He was executed on March 1, 1877, a victim of his own boastful words.

Ben Thompson spent more time on the wrong side of the law than did Wild Bill Hickok, though he, too, straddled the line. Born in 1842 in England, Thompson came to the United States in 1849 with his family and settled in Austin, Texas. A few years later he was apprenticed to a New Orleans printer, but he much preferred drinking and gambling in the town's infamous saloons.

Thompson had to cross the border to Mexico after killing a man in an argument. For two years he fought bravely for the army of Mexico's French-backed ruler, Emperor Maximilian. Upon returning to Texas, he stood trial for the earlier incident and spent two years in prison on the charge of intent to kill.

After he had served his prison term, Thomp-

*English-born Ben Thompson claimed that he always let the other man fire first in a gunfight. Nevertheless, he bested as many as 20 adversaries before his career ended in a wild shoot-out inside a Texas theater.*

son, accompanied by his brother Bill, a violent drunk, headed for the cow towns of Kansas, where gambling and whiskey occupied most of his time. In one small town in 1869, a young man walked into the saloon where Thompson was gambling and started spinning his six-shooter around recklessly. A witness recalled that the youth was

> twisting his gun around and spinning it and pointing it at various men along the bar. Suddenly I heard a shot, and this gun-flashing fellow let out a squeal. His gun flew out of his hand and went clattering off across the floor, and as he grasped his hand in pain I could see he was minus a perfectly good finger for a bullet had hit him in his gun hand.

Ben Thompson stepped toward him and said, "I never want to see you do a thing like that again, hear?" The frightened youth nodded and quickly left the saloon.

Thompson later told a friend that he never intended to kill the boy. "I just wanted to slow him down a bit before he got himself into real trouble," the gunslinger revealed.

Four years later in Ellsworth, a drunken Bill Thompson killed Sheriff Chauncey Whitney when the lawman tried to disarm him. A crowd that clamored for Bill's head quickly assembled, but Ben boldly held off the mob with a shotgun while his brother fled to safety.

Thompson's bravery and skills impressed even other gunslingers. Bat Masterson declared:

> Ben Thompson was a remarkable man in many ways, and it is doubtful if in his time there was another man living who equalled him with the pistol in a life and death struggle. He was absolutely without fear and his nerves were those of the finest steel. He shot at an adversary with the same precision and deliberation that he shot at a target.

Thompson agreed that carefulness was more important than mere speed in a gunfight. "I always make it a rule to let the other fellow fire first," he claimed.

> If a man wants to fight, I argue the question with him and try to show him how foolish it would be. If he can't be dissuaded, why, then the fun begins but I always let him have first crack. Then when I fire, you see, I have the verdict of self-defense on my side. I know that he is pretty certain in his hurry, to miss. I never do.

Thompson eventually returned to Austin, where the citizens elected him marshal. After killing a man in San Antonio, he resigned in 1882 even though a jury found him not guilty of murder.

*Tom Horn, a hired gun for the West's cattle barons, was sentenced to die for killing the 14-year-old son of a farmer. On August 6, 1903, he managed to escape from jail in Cheyenne, Wyoming, only to be recaptured a few blocks away. This photo shows Horn being led back to jail. Note the presence of bicycles—a sign of the encroachment of civilization on the Wild West.*

Two years later, on March 10, 1884, he and another gunslinger named John King Fisher returned to San Antonio. They entered the Vaudeville Variety Theater, which happened to be owned by two friends of the man Thompson had earlier killed. The men, who had vowed vengeance for their friend's death, started shooting at Thompson and Fisher. In a wild gunfight, Ben Thompson was cut down by nine bullets. Like so many other gunslingers, the Texan who had made a name with the gun—using it on both sides of the law to kill anywhere from 8 to 20 men—himself died by the gun.

Tom Horn, another gunslinger, loved to brag, "[K]illing is my specialty. I look at it as a business proposition, and I think I have a corner on the market." Though he killed under the cloak of legality, Horn basically was little more than a psychopathic murderer.

Born in 1861 in Missouri, he headed west after a bitter argument with his father and became an Indian scout for the U.S. cavalry. He helped track the Apache leader Geronimo to his Mexican hideout, where he played a crucial role in arranging for Geronimo's surrender to General Nelson Miles. Horn had learned to speak both fluent Spanish and Apache during the campaign, and he later claimed that these had been his happiest years. When the Apache wars ended in 1887, he took the job of deputy sheriff of Yavapi County, Arizona.

Beginning in 1890, Horn worked for the Pinkerton Detective Agency tracking down wanted criminals, even being so bold as to chase an outlaw right into the infamous Hole-in-the-Wall, hideout for Butch Cassidy and the Sundance Kid. Unlike other Pinkerton agents, Horn normally brought in his men dead; he supposedly

*Offered a sentence of life imprisonment in exchange for naming the wealthy cattle barons who had employed him as a killer, Tom Horn opted to face the gallows instead. He spent his last few months writing his memoirs and fashioning the rope with which he was hanged.*

killed 17 in his four years of employment with Pinkerton.

Horn next worked as a "cattle detective." Though the term implied that his job was to hunt down cattle rustlers and thieves, he actually was no more than a hired murderer for the large cattle barons, killing anyone who stood in the way of their profits. Homesteaders who would not leave rangeland the cattle barons wanted and sheep ranchers, whose animals also needed grazing land, were common targets.

Working mainly for the Swan Land and Cattle Company, Horn received $500 to $700 for each murder. Labeling himself "an exterminatin' son-of-a-gun," he used the skills he learned during the Apache campaign—patient stalking and ambush—to relentlessly pursue and kill his quarry. He sometimes waited weeks before getting a proper shot at his victim.

One cattle baron described the ruthless Horn, who differed from the other cattle detectives by always killing his foe, as a man who "classed cattle thieves with wolves and coyotes, and looked upon himself as a benefactor of society in destroying them, killing without feeling or compunction." He typically used a long-range rifle. Afterward, he placed two rocks beneath the victim's head so that when the body was found, his employers would know he had completed the job.

After serving in the Spanish-American War, Horn returned to his work for the cattle barons. It proved to be his undoing. On July 18, 1901, he set up an ambush for Kels Nickell, a local farmer who had angered the cattlemen by bringing in sheep. Horn botched the job, however, by accidentally killing Nickell's 14-year-old son Willie, whom he mistook for his target.

Even though the killing bore Horn's signature style, in the absence of any firm evidence, many in the area were content to let the matter pass. But U.S. marshal Joe LeFors refused. He followed Horn to Denver, joined him in a saloon, and, with a hidden assistant taking notes, got the drunken gunslinger to admit to the murder.

Horn bragged that cattle barons had paid him $2,100 "for killing three men and shooting five times at another" and admitted to LeFors that while killing the Nickell boy was "the dirtiest trick I have ever done," it was just part of the job. LeFors arrested Horn immediately after the conversation.

The wealthy cattlemen, fearing that Horn would divulge their names, anonymously poured thousands of dollars into his defense fund and hired the eminent lawyer John W. Lacey to defend him. In spite of this, a jury found Horn guilty of murder and sentenced him to be hanged.

While awaiting his execution, Horn received an offer to have his death sentence commuted to life imprisonment if he would identify which cattle barons had hired him. He rejected the deal—much to the relief of his former employers.

On August 6, 1903, Horn and another prisoner, Jim McCloud, managed to overpower a guard and escape. Horn got only two blocks away before being recaptured and taken back to jail in front of a mob howling for his immediate hanging. To ensure that Horn would not escape, Kels Nickell stood outside the jail with a shotgun and said, "Let Horn make another break for it and I'll blow his head off. He's going to hang if I have to stay here for the rest of my life."

In the few months remaining, Horn wrote his memoirs and laboriously fashioned the rope with which he was to be hanged. On November 20, 1903, an executioner placed the noose Horn had made around his neck, and Tom Horn fell to his death.

# EPILOGUE

*This page: Billy the Kid. Facing page: Paul Newman as Billy the Kid in* The Left Handed Gun. *Depictions of the gunslingers in movies and popular literature are largely romanticized myth.*

The Old West holds a peculiar grip on the American imagination, and central to our fascination is the figure of the gunslinger. Generations of wide-eyed readers have devoured countless books detailing the gunslingers' exploits—liberally embellished—beginning, in some cases, while the subjects were still roaming the West. And fast-draw artists, both fictional and historical, continue to play out their deadly encounters in movie theaters and on television screens. A sheriff faces down black-hatted killers at high noon . . . a gunslinger running from his past straps on his six-shooters one last time to save a family of homesteaders . . . a man with no name drifts into a corrupt western town and uses his guns to put things right. And Billy the Kid rides again, transformed from a beady-eyed, bucktoothed sociopath into a handsome, charming gunman. Shot down by Sheriff Pat Garrett, he will rise another day, on another channel.

What do we find so enthralling about the gunslingers? Is it their self-reliance, their coolness in the face of grave danger, the way they dispense an instant, unambiguous form of justice? Whatever the appeal, depictions of the gunslingers are frequently little more than romanticized myths that gloss over the coarseness, the pettiness, the drunkenness and brutality of their world. Notwithstanding the scenes of graceful, choreographed violence that are a staple of the Hollywood Western, gunslingers did not

always die instantly from a perfectly aimed shot to the head or heart. Many lingered in agony for hours or even days. And notwithstanding the Westerns' ever-present face-to-face showdowns, in which the bad guy invariably draws first, men were routinely killed from behind or from ambush. In short, the gunslingers of history often bear little resemblance to the gunslingers of our imagination.

# CHRONOLOGY

1861     The Civil War begins

1865     Wild Bill Hickok shoots Davis Tutt in a now-famous gunfight in Springfield, Missouri

1866     Hickok meets reporter H. M. Stanley, who writes an exaggerated account of his exploits and thus begins his legend

1868     John Wesley Hardin kills his first man

1871     Wild Bill Hickok becomes marshal of Abilene, Kansas, in April

1873     The Colt Peacemaker six-shooter and the Winchester Model 1873 rifle are introduced

1874     John Wesley Hardin kills Sheriff Charlie Webb, touching off a massive manhunt for the gunslinger

1875     In revenge for the ambush of his cousin, William Longley murders a rancher named Wilson Anderson

1876     Turkey Creek Jack Johnson survives a celebrated gunfight with two men in Deadwood, Dakota Territory; Doc Holliday kills a cavalryman in Texas; Wild Bill Hickok is shot from behind while playing poker in a Deadwood saloon

1877     On August 17 Billy the Kid commits his first recorded killing; John Wesley Hardin is arrested in Florida on August 23; William Longley is hanged on October 11

1878     Rancher John Tunstall, Billy the Kid's employer, is murdered on February 18, embroiling Billy in the Lincoln County, New Mexico, cattle war

1880     Sheriff Pat Garrett arrests Billy the Kid on December 26

1881     On April 28 Billy the Kid murders two guards and escapes from the Lincoln County Courthouse; Pat Garrett kills Billy the Kid on July 14; in Tombstone, Arizona, on October 26, the Earp brothers and Doc Holliday shoot it out with the Clanton-McLowery gang in what will be remembered as "the gunfight at the O. K. Corral"

1884  Ben Thompson is killed during a shoot-out in a San Antonio theater on March 10

1887  Tom Horn helps capture Geronimo; Doc Holliday dies in Colorado on November 8

1890  Tom Horn begins working as a Pinkerton agent

1894  John Wesley Hardin is pardoned after serving 17 years in prison

1895  John Wesley Hardin is killed in El Paso, Texas, on August 19

1901  On July 18 Tom Horn mistakenly shoots the 14-year-old son of a farmer he was hired to kill; he is later arrested in Denver and sentenced to be hanged for the murder

1903  Tom Horn and another prisoner briefly escape from jail on August 6; Horn is hanged on November 20

# FURTHER READING

Brown, Dee. *The American West.* New York: Touchstone, 1995.

Connelley, William E. *Wild Bill and His Era: The Life and Adventures of James Butler Hickok* (reprint). Totowa, N.J.: Cooper Square, 1972.

Cusic, Don. *Cowboys and the Wild West: An A-Z Guide from the Chisholm Trail to the Silver Screen.* New York: Facts On File, 1994.

DeArment, Robert K. *Bat Masterson: The Man and the Legend.* Norman: University of Oklahoma Press, 1979.

Horan, James D. *The Authentic Wild West: The Gunfighters.* New York: Crown Publishers, Inc., 1976.

_____. *The Authentic Wild West: The Outlaws.* New York: Crown Publishers, Inc., 1977.

McLoughlin, Denis. *Wild and Wooly: An Encyclopedia of the Old West.* Garden City, N.Y.: Doubleday & Co., Inc., 1975.

Monaghan, Jay, ed. *The Book of the American West.* New York: Julian Messner, Inc., 1963.

Myers, John M. *Doc Holliday.* Lincoln: University of Nebraska Press, 1973.

Nash, Jay Robert. *Bloodletters and Bad Men.* New York: M. Evans and Co., Inc., 1973.

_____. *Encyclopedia of Western Lawmen and Outlaws.* New York: Paragon House, 1992.

O'Neal, Bill. *Encyclopedia of Western Gunfighters.* Norman: University of Oklahoma Press, 1979.

Rosa, Joseph G. *Age of the Gunfighter.* New York: Smithmark Publishers, Inc., 1993.

Stiles, T. J. *Jesse James.* New York: Chelsea House, 1994.

Trachtman, Paul. *The Old West: The Gunfighters.* New York: Time-Life Books, 1974.

Tuska, Jon. *Billy the Kid: A Handbook.* Lincoln: University of Nebraska Press, 1986.

# INDEX

# PICTURE CREDITS

page

6: Western History Collection, University of Oklahoma Library

9: Western History Collection, University of Oklahoma Library

12: Western History Collection, University of Oklahoma Library

15: Western History Collection, University of Oklahoma Library

16: W. H. Over Museum, University of South Dakota

20: Buffalo Bill Historical Society

21: Arizona Historical Society

24: Corbis-Bettmann

27: Western History Collection, University of Oklahoma Library

29: Corbis-Bettmann

30: Western History Department, Denver Public Library

33: Western History Collection, University of Oklahoma Library

34-35: Arizona Historical Society

40: Kansas State Historical Society

43: Kansas State Historical Society

47: Archives Division, Texas State Library

49: New York Public Library

51: American Heritage Center, University of Wyoming

54: Western History Department, Denver Public Library

55: Corbis-Bettmann

# ABOUT THE AUTHOR

John F. Wukovits is a teacher and writer from Trenton, Michigan, who specializes in history and sports. His work has appeared in more than 25 national publications, including *Wild West* and *America's Civil War*. His books include a biography of the World War II commander Admiral Clifton Sprague and biographies of Barry Sanders, Vince Lombardi, and Jesse James for Chelsea House. A graduate of the University of Notre Dame, Wukovits is the father of three daughters—Amy, Julie, and Karen.